GW00986238

2

ARIZONA
A VIEW FROM ABOVE

"The airplane has unveiled for us the true face of the earth."
— Antoine de Saint-Exupéry

PHOTOGRAPHS AND TEXT BY MICHAEL COLLIER

WESTCLIFFE PUBLISHERS, INC. ENGLEWOOD, COLORADO

CONTENTS

International Standard Book Number: ISBN 0-929969-34-0
Library of Congress Catalogue Card Number: 89-52044
Copyright, Photographs and Text: Michael Collier, 1990.
 All rights reserved.
Editor: John Fielder
Assistant Editor: Margaret Terrell Morse
Production Manager: Mary Jo Lawrence
Typographers: Richard M. Kohen & Dianne J. Borneman
Printed in Singapore by Tien Wah Press, Ltd.
Published by Westcliffe Publishers, Inc.
 2650 South Zuni Street
 Englewood, Colorado 80110

Bibliography

Abbey, Edward. *The Journey Home*. New York: E.P. Dutton, 1977. Reprinted with permission.
 Edward Abbey spent much of his life living in and writing about his beloved Southwest. A naturalist and storyteller, he was an eloquent and controversial supporter of the environment in his fiction and nonfiction writings.

"Painting with Child" (pp. 86-87), "Before the Light is Steady" (pp. 82, 84), and "The Level Eye" (pp. 90, 92-94) by Lucille Adler from *The Ripening Light: Selected Poems 1977-1987* (Gibbs Smith, Publisher/Peregrine Smith Books; 1989). Reprinted with permission.
 Lucille Adler is a 20th-century poet whose work is deeply influenced by the Southwest, where she makes her home. As May Sarton once wrote, "Lucille Adler gives us poems as hermetic and open as Georgia O'Keefe's landscapes that haunt for the same reason, plain and mysterious, rich in their austerities."

Krutch, Joseph Wood. *The Desert Year*. New York: William Sloane Associates, 1951-52. Reprinted with permission.
 Joseph Wood Krutch was a 20th-century critic, biographer, naturalist and teacher. A frequent traveler to Arizona, he wrote *The Desert Year* while on a 15-month sabbatical living in the Sonoran desert outside of Tucson.

Udall, Stewart. *The Quiet Crisis and the Next Generation*. Layton, Utah: Gibbs Smith, 1988.
 Arizona native Stewart Udall is a former secretary of the Interior and a onetime Arizona congressman. An avid environmentalist, he has numerous books to his credit.

First Frontispiece: *Baboquivari Mountains and a distant Kitt Peak, along the eastern border of the Papago Indian Reservation*
Second Frontispiece: *Apache Lake glistens in early morning sun, along the Salt River*

Title Page: *Aspen changing color, San Francisco Peaks*
Right: *Patterns along the Colorado River, Cibola National Wildlife Refuge*

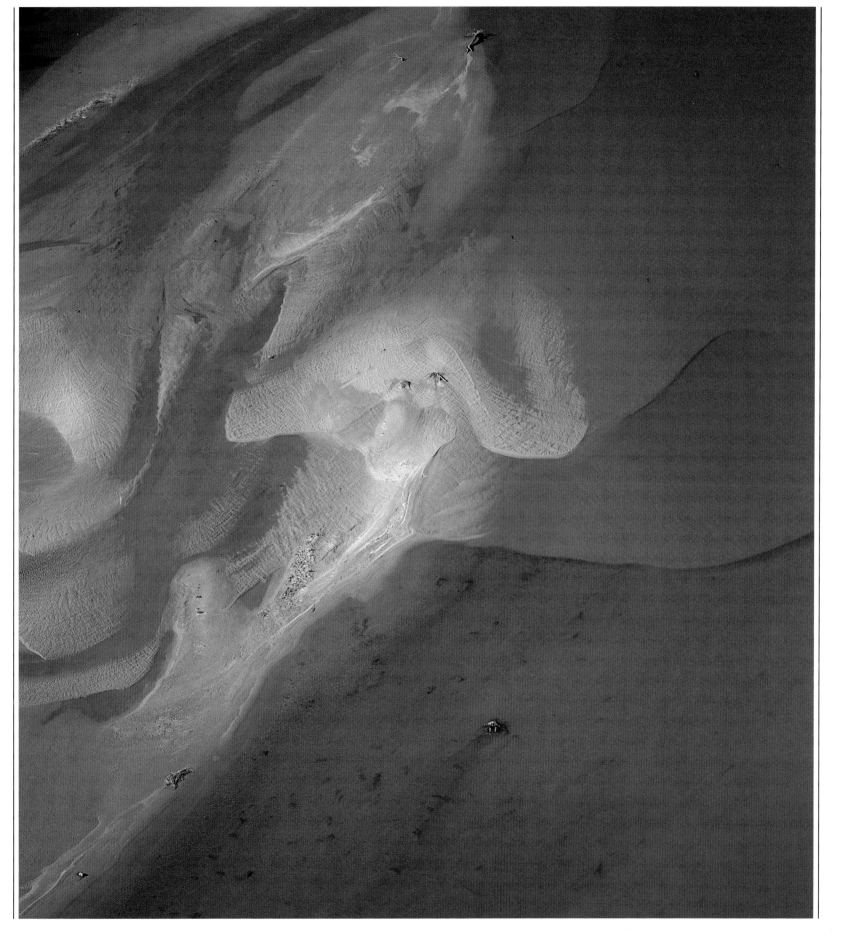

FOREWORD

To fully appreciate a western landscape, you should see it from the air. Take the Grand Canyon. When you look down from the rim in the national park, the view is certainly spectacular, but still a little unreal, like looking at a museum diorama through a pane of glass. Somehow it is too large; you can't imagine where it begins or ends, or how it came to exist in the first place.

One way to see the whole is to take a flight from Los Angeles to Chicago. About 30 minutes out you will see Lake Mead off to the right, an incongruous blue pond right there in the midst of a gritty expanse of sand and clay and rock. Follow the eastern finger of the lake up to where it pokes through the Grand Wash Cliffs and you will find the mouth of the canyon.

For the next 20 minutes you can trace the entire 300-mile course of the Colorado River as it twists across northern Arizona. The lower third, upstream from Lake Mead to Kanab Canyon, is a chaotic landscape, a junk-yard of erosional remnants cut to shreds by gulleys and side canyons. Then, as the river cuts headward across the emerald forests of the Kaibab, you see the classic Grand Canyon, where the rims drop straight off, revealing an orderly, architectural procession of temples and buttes. Finally, across the Kaibab, the river suddenly bends northward and disappears from sight in the narrow, shadowy trench of Marble Canyon, and you are across the river headed toward the Rocky Mountains.

After seeing the entire Grand Canyon from the air, go back to the national park and walk up to the rim again. This time the postcard vistas will make sense, for you will see them as scenes in a pattern of time, a flowing river and the structure of the great plateaus.

To be sure, there are places on the ground where you can get an aerial perspective and begin to feel the space and structure of the desert. For a beginning, try the rimrock views at the edge of the plateaus where the rock layers have been stripped away by erosion. Look down several thousand feet to where another layer emerges and then runs off toward infinity. Try Nankoweap in the autumn when you can look through the yellowing aspen groves onto the Marble Platform. Stay until sunset when the light show begins and you will see that even infinite horizons have limits. To the north the Paria Cliffs turn deep red. To the east the Echo Cliffs flame crimson.

And to the south the San Francisco Peaks, purple and blue, seem to levitate above the land. Or go to the very edge of the Hopi Mesas on a summer day, as cloud shadows drift across the plains, setting the desert floor in motion like the sea itself. If you remain here until dusk, the distant, darkening Hopi Buttes will rise up like sailing ships floating in a sea of blue.

The problem is that even at the Grand Canyon the landscapes are threatened by dirty air and misplaced development. The air is losing its sparkle as plumes of sulfur dioxide from power plants saturate the skies. The land is strip-mined for coal, the volcanic hills are bulldozed for aggregate, and the precious few remaining streams are deranged in the name of progress.

When I became governor in 1978 I decided to see what could be done about preserving the last of the remote open spaces that are so distinctive a feature of Arizona. I called in the land commissioner and together we spread out a map of the land ownership patterns of the state. What we saw was a crazy quilt pattern of colors—green for National Forest Service, yellow for Bureau of Land Management, blue for state of Arizona, orange for Indian reservations, red for military reservations and purple for national parks, all interspersed with white squares for private lands descended from old land grants and homestead entries. If the intermixed private lands continued to be sold off as subdivisions, Arizona eventually would look like New Jersey or Iowa, with hardly a single unimpaired, wide open space where you could stand and experience the freedom of a true frontier. We decided right then and there to undertake an exchange program to block up the back country into permanent, unimpaired public ownership. We could do that by trading publicly held lands near the urban areas for key rural tracts that should remain free of development.

Our first big project was to create a corridor of permanent public reserves along the San Pedro River, one of the few remaining desert streams in the state. We began by exchanging into public ownership the old Spanish land grants along the river, acquiring additional lands adjacent to the national forest in the Galiuro Mountains and exchanging lands in the tributaries of Aravaipa Canyon into federal ownership and from there into wilderness status. These trades involved the Bureau of Land Management, the state, the Nature Conservancy and private owners; the result was a great strip of protected lands running from the Mexican border clear up to the Gila River.

We then turned to northern Arizona to acquire old homesteads along Oak Creek Canyon, an area that might well have qualified for national park status if we could have turned the clock back 100 years. At Sliderock and Fry Ranch we now have state parks, instead of trailer parks and condominiums blocking access to the water. In the Verde Valley we initiated a similar program of acquiring riparian lands in the great cottonwood forests that stretch from Tuzigoot down to Bridgeport. We then moved the program to other parts of the state.

Today this process of rearranging the land map of Arizona to preserve open space is continuing under the leadership of the Bureau of Land Management and the Nature Conservancy. Ultimately, if it is successful, Arizona will continue to have big open spaces, with development concentrated in distinct cities and towns, proving that we can have growth as well as a beautiful natural environment. The alternative is that random sprawl, all too common in the West, that consumes and obliterates the natural landscape. In this book, Michael Collier, with camera and airplane, gives us an eloquent testimonial to the importance of this task.

— BRUCE BABBITT
Governor of Arizona, 1978–1987

9

Brush and rock patterns, northern end of the Dragoon Mountains

Overleaf: *Nature sculpts stone in Monument Valley Navajo Tribal Park, Arizona/Utah border*

INTRODUCTION

Roger Henderson and I tighten our seatbelts and settle onto runway one-one at Tucson International. Like marsh hawks, we have just spent two hours gliding stiff-winged above open ground, hunting. The plane twisted this way then that, graceful in the early morning light, aligning itself with an image of cottonwoods along the Santa Cruz River, of limestone ledges in the Mescal Mountains. Hunting with our eyes.

Could there be a more refined joy?—warm air tumbling in torrents through the open window, wheeling across a brilliant clear sky, exploring Arizona. Roger is a sucker for this state. So am I. Neither born, but both raised here. Each of us has spent the greater part of three decades wandering its back roads—Roger as a sometimes-archeologist, I as a gentleman geologist, both as photographers.

Arizona has shown me many faces—on foot in the Catalinas, astride a horse in the Mazatzals, bicycling through Yarnell, locked into a kayak on the upper Salt, leaning out a boxcar door rolling through Ash Fork. Chrysotile, Bagdad and Bisbee; Sasabe, Seba Dalkai and the San Pedro. I have always been enthralled by the smell of creosote after a desert rain, by

Hah Ho No Gah Canyon, east of Tuba City

the sound of wind through ponderosas, by the sight of sunrise washing across the San Francisco Peaks. These deserts and forests, canyons and mountains, have grown into my bones, lodged themselves in my eye. This land, this Arizona, flows like blood, like a river, through my heart. It is my home.

Once on the ground, it is not so obvious that I am hopelessly in love with Arizona; I uncoil from the cockpit, single-mindedly looking for avgas and a bathroom. I'm scruffy, face smudged with a two-day stubble. My eyes are red, wind-scratched after hanging out the window while Roger flew. Roger climbs out the other door, grumbling about the heat.

My plane, affectionately named the Buzzard, is a high-winged taildragger that has only one ambition—to fly and then fly some more. The paint is peeling and mud is splattered over both struts and the elevator. Last night Roger and I camped beneath its wings outside of Superior. A stiff wind rose after sundown. With no convenient place to tie the plane down, I reached up out of my sleeping bag, hung a line down from the wing and tied it around my waist. Human ballast. Every 15 or 20 minutes I was jerked three inches off the ground by a fresh blast of wind.

In the morning I grinned to see Roger beneath the other wing, untying a similar line and rubbing the bruises in the small of his back. We dusted ourselves off and set out to see more of this state—rising above Superior, turning down to the Dripping Spring Mountains, working our way along the Galiuro and Winchester mountains, ending up in Tucson, waiting out the day until we could fly in the rich light of sunset.

If Hollywood were to be believed, the essence of Arizona would be a silent cowboy moseying past saguaro cactus silhouetted against a flaming sunset in Monument Valley. But the Duke is dead, and there never were saguaros in Monument Valley. Arizona is much more than the sum of its stereotyped parts. Over the years I have come to see the state as the melding of five landscapes, each presented as a chapter in this book.

The southern deserts host a tremendous biologic diversity. The Sonoran desert sweeps up out of Mexico, its cactus, palo verde and creosote covering the lowlands of southern Arizona from sea level to a bit over 3,000 feet. This is the land of balmy winters and murderous summers, where the bulk of the state's population lives. At its higher elevations, this desert gives way to chaparral and grassland, dotted with scrub oak and manzanita.

The deserts and grasslands of southern Arizona are overlain by a second landscape—mountains that rise like islands above the shimmering heat of the desert floor. Their summits rise 9,000 and 10,000 feet into a world of cool misty mornings and plentiful rainfall.

The Mogollon Rim defines a third sector of the state. This irregular green wall stands almost 8,000 feet above sea level, slashing diagonally northwest to southeast across the state. From the Rim and its associated highlands flow the Little Colorado, Verde, Blue, Black and White rivers, and then the Salt.

The high deserts of the reservation country and the Arizona Strip lie north of the Mogollon Rim. Here pinyon and juniper grow where they can, sagebrush and sand where they cannot. It is home to the Navajo in their hogans, the Hopi on their mesa-tops. Here the horizon lies 100 miles away.

Finally, there is the canyon country. Its abysses are carved in a thousand different patterns,

13

creating within the high deserts a mirror image of the southern mountains that rise up out of the Sonoran desert. In this canyonscape, sunlight is given a million different reflections, and imagination knows no bounds.

Arizona is an aerial photographer's paradise. The weather is usually best described as "severe clear." The colors of the landscape are infinitely varied. Most important, there is the topography: mountains, ridges, mesas, canyons, chasms, cliffs, rims, plateaus, buttes, valleys, spires. From above, Arizona's landscape reads like front page headlines.

I've always been fascinated by the fabric of landscape seen from 35,000 feet. In a commercial airliner I'm as guilty as any six-year-old of jamming my nose against the window from takeoff to landing: a happy Plexiglas prisoner. But as my own pilot, I gain the freedom to swoop down, open the window and examine every stitch and seam of the land.

At its best, aerial photography is an oblique exploration of the third dimension. Landscape that once existed only within the realms of north and south, east and west, suddenly expands. Topography takes on a new significance. Lifting off the runway, a photographer

*S̸and dunes bear
evidence of
ceaseless winds,
Monument Valley
Navajo Tribal Park*

is free to integrate one more variable—that third dimension—into his vision of the world.

From 12,000 feet, Arizona is less of a geographic hodgepodge than from below. The kaleidoscopic changes of vegetation—pine to sagebrush to saguaro—make more sense. Rivers drop out of mountains through canyons and then past broad valleys on their way to the Sea of Cortez. The transitions of high deserts through Rim country to southern deserts become more orderly from an overhead perspective. On the ground, a snowstorm over my home in Flagstaff seems to engulf the entire world. But from the air, I see instead that the storm feathers out to blue sky over Kingman. The world is more connected, less insular than I might have otherwise thought.

This newfound perspective is not without its own complexities and responsibilities. Most obviously, you can't crash. And you aren't allowed to run out of film. Either would spoil everything.

All photographers must learn to orchestrate the interplay of mechanics—film speed, exposure values, focal length—with the aesthetics of photography—light, color, contrast, composition, content. Pilots experience a similar interplay—concerning themselves on one hand with oil pressure, airspeed, fuel consumption, navigation—and on the other hand with the special beauty of the world that is around and below them. Aerial photographers live at the crossroads of all these considerations. The rate-limiting step in my photography is all too often my limited ability to integrate so much information so fast. But it's fun to try: hanging out the window behind the camera, fine-tuning the plane's angle with my feet, smoke pouring out my ears.

A backup pilot is an obvious solution.

Roger, Jim Harkreader, Ed Peacock, Richard Jackson, Chris Condit—their enthusiasms and abilities outweigh their depletion of my motion-sickness doggy-bag supply. But even with the best of help, a photographer must never be content to really let another pilot fly him anywhere: that would be like taking a Greyhound to Grand Canyon and letting the bus driver choose the site to set up the tripod.

For better or worse, aerial photography is as tightly bound to its machinery as any art form can be. Motor-driven, auto-exposure cameras are indispensable. A surefooted knowledge of the range and limitations of your film is mandatory. And it helps to have a good airplane between you and the ground.

The Buzzard, bless its heart, was born 35 years ago, bred to this life of dirt strips and tight turns. As a STOL-equipped taildragger, it is perfectly willing to drop in on some short, rough strip while I brew a cup of coffee and wait out the angle of the sun, the quality of the light. The Buzzard knows more about flying than I ever will.

In some circles, small airplanes have become a symbol of freedom: the unfettering of earth's chains, free as a bird, the sky's the limit. By and large, that is all nonsense. Small planes are ghastly expensive. And once you get somewhere, you've still got to figure out how to get anywhere beyond the airport. Flying from airport coffee shop to airport coffee shop is hardly my idea of ultimate freedom.

But if you look carefully, there is freedom in flight: The freedom to see the world from an infinite number of new perspectives. The freedom to decide that the light within a canyon might be better photographed from *that* rim than from *this* rim. The freedom to contrapose this mountain up against that plateau.

15

16

Or the freedom to just fly and soak it all in and not take any photographs at all.

The greatest joy of aerial photography is to experience those moments when everything flows together, when all the butterflies in your stomach are flying in formation. The light is just right, the airplane is flying perfectly, and you are free to create images from a vantage point that may have never been seen before.

Above the Vermilion Cliffs your mind's eye frames a wall of red and gray and gold and green. Drop down a bit, nose into a left bank, roll out, check the oil pressure, watch the light on the cliffs, anticipate the shutter speed and aperture, lift the wing and square the horizon, follow the composition in the view-finder, steady the camera against the air's tur-bulence and *photograph* until the bearings in your motor drive are screeching, then look up at the cliff that is coming into your windshield. Roll out hard to the right, check your airspeed and oil pressure, and do it all over again, but this time, oh, maybe 75 feet lower. Four or five hours of this sort of flying leave me exhilarated and utterly drained. Art in the fast lane.

Early morning sun over western Grand Canyon National Park, near Toroweap Point

There is a change that threatens the beauty that I have found above Arizona, a change that I have tried desperately not to show in these photographs. Our air is no longer clear. I remember Phoenix through a child's eyes in the late 1950s, when I could regularly see the Bradshaw Mountains in razor-sharp focus. Peaks 50 miles away stood in stark relief against the blue sky behind them. Nowadays even the smudged and muted form of these mountains is a rare sight from Phoenix, let alone the fine details I saw years ago on their slopes. Those Bradshaw ridgelines have been replaced by a cancerous brown smear that blots the Arizona horizon for a hundred or more miles downwind from Phoenix. Time and again, flying across the state's midriff at 8,000 or 10,000 feet, I have had to stare straight ahead, pretend I don't see the brown haze that strangles the Superstition Moun-tains, swallow back that old bitterness that I feel rising up in my throat.

Who is responsible for this degradation of the air we breathe? To be sure, Los Angeles and Tucson each contribute a share. The cop-per producers and power companies begrudg-ingly install scrubbers at their smelters in San Manuel and Douglas, electrostatic precipi-tators at their coal-fired plants in Page, Joseph City and Saint Johns—decreasing but not halt-ing the emission of sulfates, ash and other pollutants into the air. Oxidative agents are added to gasoline in an attempt to reduce ozone contamination from automobiles. Still the air quality declines.

A few folks use the smoke-screen argument that blames "natural causes"—dust or pine tree resins. To do so is to ask me and others who lived in Arizona 30 years ago to forget the truths of our younger days. Other folks are quick to singularly blame this plant or that smelter for all of our woes. But I suspect that shrill name-calling and environmental finger-pointing will be no more effective than rearranging the deck chairs on the Titanic, until we are all willing to make a real-life commitment to cleaner air. It will take money directly out of my wallet and yours—in the form of higher prices for electricity and sub-sidies for viable mass-transit systems. It will require rearranging our priority of growth-at-all-costs, thereby living without the very real benefits of some forms of industry that in the long run just aren't worth the air-quality costs that they incur. And it will mean standing up to our upwind neighbors, demanding that they stop exporting their pollution to us.

One morning when I first started working on this book, I awoke from a dream in a cold sweat. I had been flying—near Kingman, I believe—and I could find no open ground. There were only houses, one just like the other, stretching out to and beyond the horizon. Each house had a swimming pool, two cars and a tidy lawn. I sat up in bed, shivered and tried to shake off that image of a devastation yet to come. What was there left to photo-graph? Where was there space left to breathe?

This book bears witness that my dream has not come to pass. Phoenix and Tucson con-tinue to expand, but fortunately, more than 80 percent of Arizona is publicly owned or controlled, and the land is still largely un-spoiled. After 15 years of flying, after 1,000 hours and 100,000 miles across the Arizona sky, I have found here a wealth of solitude, entire worlds of open space. These photo-graphs celebrate the survival of the tremen-dous wilderness that is still Arizona.

—MICHAEL COLLIER

17

Dedicated to Roger Henderson—he has shown all of us doctors a thing or two about the bravest kind of flying.

Southern Deserts

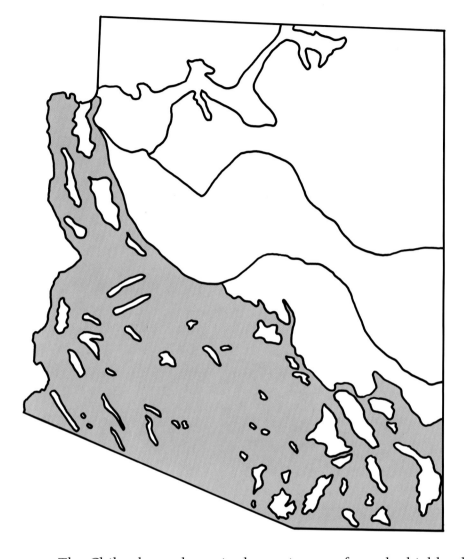

To many folks, Arizona *is* the desert. Actually, it is more: southern Arizona is made up of three deserts—the Mojave to the west, the Chihuahuan to the east and the Sonoran in between. They share a common denominator—all receive less than 10 inches of rainfall per year. The distinctions among the three are subtle, based primarily on botanic assemblages. I use a simplified system: if saguaro cacti are nearby, I am on (or above) the Sonoran desert.

The Mojave desert is a California import. Only a small portion of it crosses the Colorado River into Arizona. Creosote bush and bursage dominate hillsides, which are given only sporadically to exuberances like the comical Joshua tree and the evanescent spring blooms of the California poppy.

The Chihuahuan desert is also an import, from the highlands of the Mexican state of Chihuahua. Only one-quarter of this desert lies within Arizona. Average elevation is 3,000 to 5,000 feet, and annual precipitation varies from eight to 10 inches. These two factors make Arizona's Chihuahuan desert an excellent grassland, dotted with scrub oak and a few mesquite trees.

The Sonoran desert is the largest of Arizona's southern deserts, stretching from Tucson to the Colorado River, and from Phoenix past the border well into its namesake Mexican state, Sonora. Here cactus is king. Specifically, saguaro cactus. This 20-ton giant is quickly brought to its knees by any significant frost. The Sonoran desert, consequently, tends to be restricted to elevations between sea level and a bit over 3,000 feet.

After defining the western border of Arizona, the Colorado River flows into the Sea of Cortez, Baja California

*P*alo verdes
along
20   *McClellan Wash,
east of
Newman Peak*

*agle Creek
flows around
the eastern end
of the
Gila Mountains,
west of Clifton*   21

Overleaf:
*Santa Rita
foothills, above
Sonoita Creek*

𝓜eanders of the Verde River, above Tangle Creek along
the western edge of the Mazatzal Wilderness

Chevron ridges of tilted sedimentary rock, west of Pierce Ferry
in Lake Mead National Recreation Area

"Here, the contest is not so much of plant against plant
as of plant against inanimate nature. The limiting
factor is not the neighbor but water; . . . that is,
perhaps, one of the things which makes this country
seem to enjoy a kind of peace one does not find
elsewhere. The struggle of living thing against living
thing can be distressing in a way that a mere battle
with the elements is not." —Joseph Wood Krutch

Galiuro foothills north of Redfield Canyon, above the San Pedro River

Salt River, at Gleason Flats

"*There is no continuous carpet of grass or herbage, no crowding together of exuberantly growing plant life. One does not push one's way through undergrowth; one strolls almost as in a garden. Where water is scarce, roots spread far and shallowly. . . . Because of a spacing which nature has attended to, it has a curious air of being a park rather than a wilderness.*"
—Joseph Wood Krutch

*S*anta Rita foothills, above Sonoita Creek

*Colorado River patterns, downstream from the
Cibola National Wildlife Refuge*

"*That the desert here is mildly austere is certainly
true, and yet neither the plants nor the animals live
under what is, for them, painfully difficult conditions.
The vegetation flourishes in its own way. For the desert
birds and the desert animals . . . this is obviously a
paradise and there is no paradox in the smile which
the face of the desert wears.*" —Joseph Wood Krutch

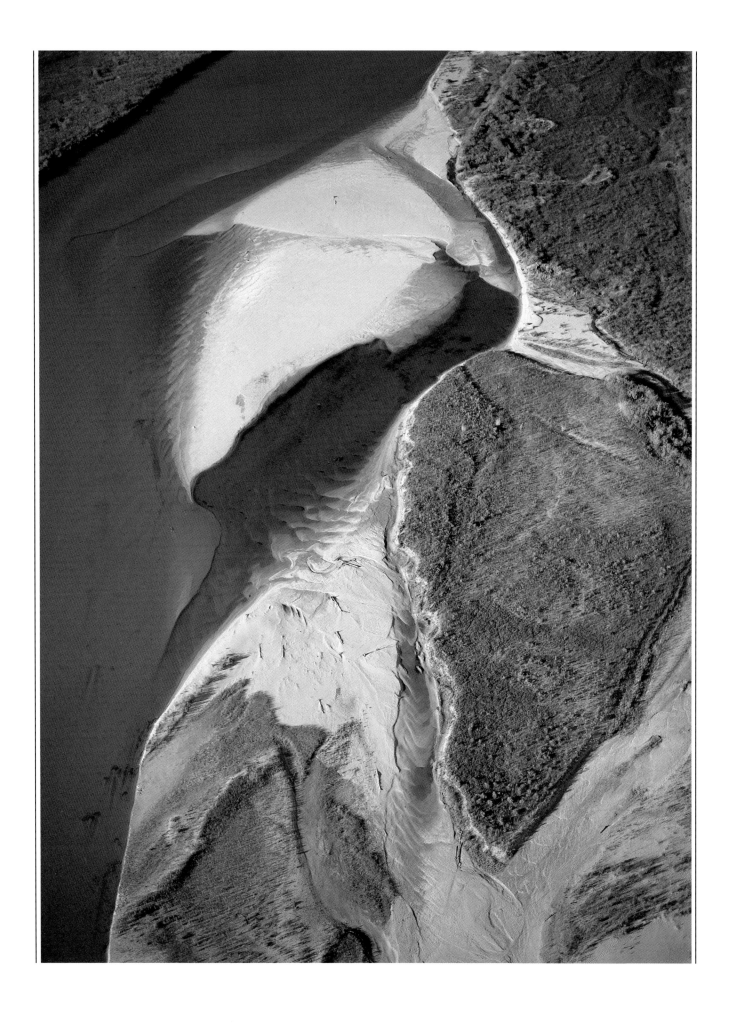

*G*aliuro foothills north of Redfield Canyon,
above the San Pedro River

Salt River, at Gleason Flats

"There is no continuous carpet of grass or herbage, no
crowding together of exuberantly growing plant life.
One does not push one's way through undergrowth;
one strolls almost as in a garden. Where water is
scarce, roots spread far and shallowly. . . . Because of
a spacing which nature has attended to, it has a
curious air of being a park rather than a wilderness."
—Joseph Wood Krutch

Foothills of the Buckskin Mountains, above the Bill Williams River

Colorado River delta, Baja California south of Yuma

"Yesterday, when I stood on a peak and looked down at an arid emptiness, . . . there was no visible evidence that the earth was inhabited. . . . Not to have known—as most men have not—either the mountain or the desert is not to have known one's self."
—Joseph Wood Krutch

*D*ry bed of Burro Creek, above Alamo Lake

Western slope of the Black Mountains, north of Bullhead City

Overleaf: Tortilla Mountains, above the Gila River Valley

"*Though bare, jagged mountains ultimately close
nearly every vista, the desert itself lies peaceful in the
sun and repeats with tireless satisfaction its two
themes—either cactus, paloverde, mesquite, and sand,
or yucca, agave, and ocotillo, the one on the flats, the
other on the slopes.*" —Joseph Wood Krutch

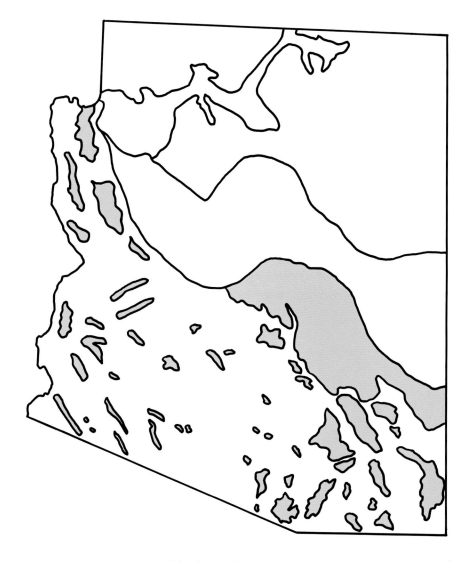

Mountain Islands

"The Islands." At first blush, it sounds like the achingly incongruous name for yet another Phoenix condominium development. But the mountain islands are an integral part of the southern Arizona landscape. Like jostling icebergs, these ranges bob up from desert basins: the Chiricahuas, the Catalinas and the Santa Ritas rise more than 9,000 feet above sea level; Mount Graham of the Pinaleno Mountains stands at 10,713 feet.

The evergreen and fern forests atop these mountains are a world unto themselves. Air cools 3 or 4 degrees for every thousand feet of elevation gained above the surrounding deserts; this translates to a temperature drop of 30 degrees from Safford to the top of Mount Graham, only 10 miles to the southwest. This cooling, in turn, is responsible for a dramatic increase in moisture—from less than 10 inches on the deserts to some 30 inches per year at the higher summits. Temperature and moisture—together their influence has led to the evolution of completely different environments isolated on top of many of southern Arizona's mountains. They have become islands of pine and aspen, awash in a sea of cactus and creosote on the deserts below.

If you squint at a topographic map of southern Arizona, an interesting alignment emerges: on average, the mountain ranges are parallel, running northwest to southeast. Between them lie the desert basins. This landscape of alternating basins and ranges is the result of extensional forces that pulled apart southern Arizona (as well as parts of California, Sonora and New Mexico) some 18 to 20 million years ago. The ranges are trimmed by faults, along which the basins have fallen and the mountains have risen. This Basin and Range is a formal geologic province that extends through Nevada and into southern Oregon and Idaho, where the faulting and mountain-building occurred much more recently.

Baboquivari Peak with Kitt Peak in the background, Baboquivari Mountains

Fumbled ridges of the Whetstone Mountains, north of Sierra Vista

38

ocky cliffs
of the
Ajo Range,
Organ Pipe Cactus
National
Monument   39

Overleaf: *Sunset*
silhouettes
Baboquivari Peak,
southwest of Tucson

*Eroded rock formations in the Superstition Mountains,
above Pine Creek*

Mustang Mountains, northwest of Sierra Vista

*"I know that many besides myself have felt [this land's]
charm, but I know also that not all who visit it do, that
there are, indeed, some in whom it inspires at first
sight not love but fear, or even hatred."*
—Joseph Wood Krutch

Superstition Mountains, within the Superstition Wilderness

Weaver's Needle, Superstition Mountains

"[This land's] appeal is not the appeal of things
universally attractive, like smiling fields, bubbling
springs, and murmuring brooks. To some it seems
merely stricken, and even those of us who love it
recognize that its beauty is no easy one."
—Joseph Wood Krutch

45

*C*louds drift over Buckhorn Mountain, west of Roosevelt Lake

Sunlight and shadow, Baboquivari Peak

"[This land] suggests patience and struggle and endurance. It is courageous and happy, not easy or luxurious. In the brightest colors of its sandstone canyons, even in the brightest colors of its brief spring flowers, there is something austere." —Joseph Wood Krutch

*M*ountains above Box Canyon, Gila River

"... man has not here utterly upset the balance of
nature, and that balance establishes itself at a level of
low density for plants, for animals, and for men.
Water gives out before anything else does, long before
there is simply no more room, and the human
population ... is inevitably spread as thin as the
desert flowers." —Joseph Wood Krutch

$\mathcal{L}$imestone ridges, Whetstone Mountains

Overleaf: *Morning light on the Whetstone Mountains,*
north of Sierra Vista

". . . the water will go only so far, even with the
mountain dams and the long canals, and the demand
for living space will have to be frustrated in other,
more easily over-exploitable regions before the dreams
of the boosters are realized as the nightmares such
dreams have a way of turning into." —Joseph Wood Krutch

51

Morning light, Ajo Range along the eastern edge of Organ Pipe Cactus National Monument

Mountains above Box Canyon, Gila River

*"To many who are accustomed to teeming lands . . .
the desert seem[s] niggardly, but to some others her
balance soon comes to seem as normal as any other.
There is no absolute standard by which one may
determine just how many plants, how many cattle, or
how many men an acre should support, and there is
much to be said in favor of elbowroom."*
—Joseph Wood Krutch

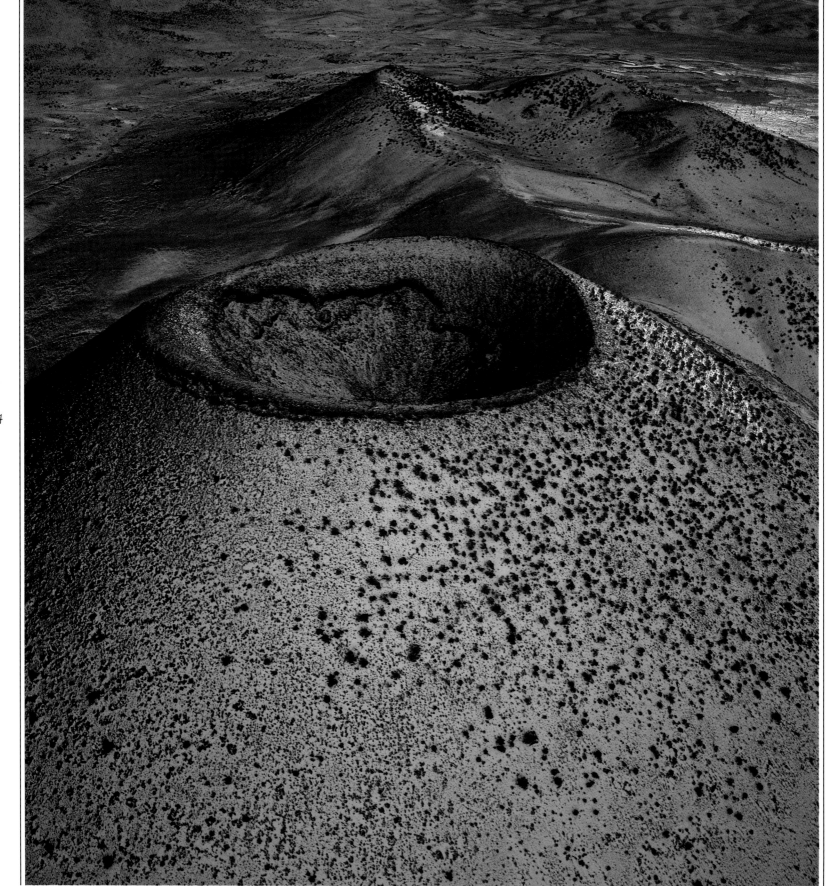

54

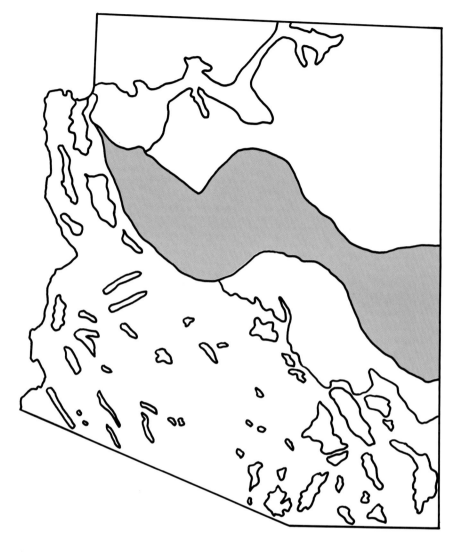

Rim Country

Arizona sits astride two major geologic provinces—the Basin and Range in the south, and the Colorado Plateau in the north. The Rim country, a diagonal swath of highlands running roughly northwest to southeast, neatly bisects Arizona and defines the boundary between the two provinces.

For the most part, the Rim is the upturned edge of the sedimentary layers that make up the Colorado Plateau, here decorated with a frosting of volcanoes and cinder hills. Its most prominent expression is the Mogollon Rim, a 1,500-foot wall running 160 miles from Perkinsville on the Verde River through McNary in the White Mountains. Elsewhere the Rim is a hodgepodge of blocks, all tilting this way and that, all significantly uplifted above the desert floor below.

Volcanic activity is apparent in many places along the Rim—the San Francisco Peaks, the White Mountains and the sheets of basalt above the Verde Valley. Sunset Crater, north of Flagstaff, erupted less than a thousand years ago—less than the blink of an eye on a geologic time scale.

Even though relatively few people live along the Rim, a tremendous amount of the state's wealth has flowed from it. First and foremost: water. The Verde, Salt and Gila rivers all flow out of or along stretches of the Rim. Most of the state's major mineral resources have been discovered nearby in the mines of Bagdad, Jerome, Superior, Globe, Ray and Morenci. And the Rim is host to the largest ponderosa pine forest in the world.

S.P. Crater, north of Flagstaff

*A*spen of the
White
*Mountains, above
Big Bonito Creek*

Springerville volcanic field, west of Eagar

Overleaf: *Aspen mark the height of autumn, San Francisco Peaks*

57

58

C louds spilling across Agassiz Peak, north of Flagstaff within the Kachina Peaks Wilderness

Sun and snow accent a conifer forest, San Francisco Peaks

"Once the southern wall of that plateau which covers almost the whole northern half of Arizona has been climbed, a different world appears. For one thing, the altitudes range from about five thousand to more than twelve thousand feet; for another, the topography and the geology are predominantly different."
—Joseph Wood Krutch

Crater at Springerville volcanic field, west of Eagar

"... the Colorado Plateau—is something special.
Something strange, marvelous, full of wonders. . . .
Nowhere else have we had this lucky combination
of vast sedimentary rock formations exposed to
a desert climate, a great plateau carved by major
rivers—the Green, the San Juan, the Colorado—into
such a surreal land of form and color." —Edward Abbey

*L*ate afternoon sun on a cinder cone, west of S.P. Crater

"Add a few volcanoes, the standing necks of which can still be seen, and cinder cones and lava flows, and at least four separate laccolithic mountain ranges nicely distributed about the region, and more hills, holes, humps and hollows, reefs, folds, salt domes, swells and grabens, buttes, benches and mesas, . . . and you begin to arrive at an approximate picture of the plateau's surface appearance." —Edward Abbey

*A*spen boles, San Francisco Peaks

Hills and ridges, east of Sedona

". . . *Wordsworth and Thoreau . . . realized that the
rare moment is not the moment when there is
something worth looking at but the moment when we
are capable of seeing.*" —Joseph Wood Krutch

65

*B*uildup of cumulonimbus clouds, northern Arizona

"For a week, perhaps, I . . . saw, a few miles away, the
lazy unraveling of some patch of nimbus as its
moisture dropped slowly to earth. Then one day our
time came. The lightning moved closer; the thunder
roared in our very ears; and, finally, the huge drops
beat down viciously, leaving little craters in the sand
where they fell." —Joseph Wood Krutch

*D*oney Fault at Wupatki National Monument, north
of the San Francisco Peaks

"The way in which both desert and plateau use form
and color is as different from the way in which more
conventionally picturesque regions use them, as the
way of the modern painter is different from that of the
academician." —Joseph Wood Krutch

*R*emnant of snow on Sunset Crater, Sunset Crater
National Monument

Cinder hill north of Sunset Crater, Sunset Crater National Monument

Overleaf: *Dusting of snow, San Francisco Peaks*

"A picture framed by sky and time in the world of natural
appearances, . . . the landscape of the Colorado Plateau
lies still beyond the reach of reasonable words. Or
unreasonable representation. This is a landscape that has
to be seen to be believed, and even then, confronted directly
by the senses, it strains credulity." —Edward Abbey

$\mathscr{A}$spen complete seasonal cycle, San Francisco Peaks

"For more and more of those who now live here,
however, the great plateau and its canyon wilderness is
a treasure best enjoyed through the body and spirit . . .
not through commercial plunder. It is a regional,
national and international treasure too valuable to be
sacrificed for temporary gain, too rare to be withheld
from our children." —Edward Abbey

S̸pringerville volcanic field, above Carnero Creek

*"For us the wilderness and human emptiness of this land
is not a source of fear but the greatest of its attractions.
We would guard and defend and save it as a place for all
who wish to rediscover the nearly lost pleasures of
adventure, adventure not only in the physical sense, but
also mental, spiritual, moral, aesthetic and intellectual
adventure. A place for the free." —Edward Abbey*

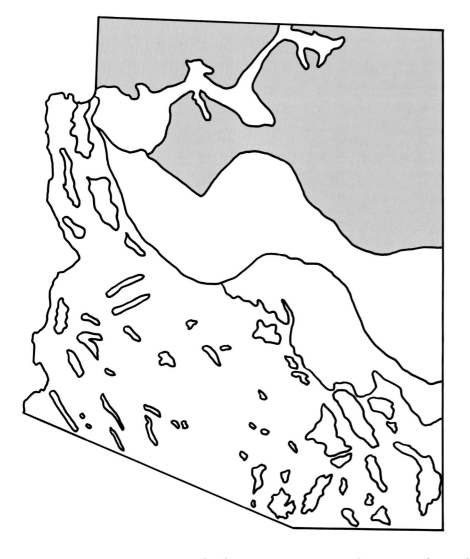

High Deserts

The high deserts of northeastern Arizona are quintessential Colorado Plateau landscape: layered sedimentary rocks, creased here and there by folds or faults, punctuated by the odd volcano, but otherwise left pretty much undisturbed by the forces that elsewhere have rototilled the earth's crust in western North America.

This is the land of sandstone cliffs and shale valleys. Erosion, working over thousands of years, has laboriously carved a fine fretwork texture throughout this country. Color permeates every panorama. The high deserts, 5,000, 6,000, 7,000 feet above sea level, are blessed by a light that, as C.E. Dutton wrote, seems to "glow from within."

A thousand years ago this land was home to the Anasazi—300,000 people, by some estimates, living on the Colorado Plateau around what are now the Four Corners of Arizona, Utah, Colorado and New Mexico. Barely that many people live here now. The Anasazi vanished just before A.D. 1300, leaving us a heritage of beautiful masonry and pottery, bequeathing to us a sense of history that stretches back well before the European exploration of eastern North America. The Hopi, probably descendants of these earlier people, still live on their mesa-tops; they were joined 500 years ago by the Navajo, living in scattered hogans, following a more migratory way of life.

Today the high deserts, with their sedimentary treasures of coal and uranium, are the focus of a great deal of economic and environmental concern. We struggle to balance our love for places like Monument Valley, Canyon de Chelly and the Painted Desert with the reality of needing the mineral resources that lie within this country.

Rock formations in Monument Valley Navajo Tribal Park, Arizona/Utah border

75

Erosion dissects the sedimentary ridges of Hah Ho No Gah Canyon, east of Tuba City

Deep shadows accentuate cliffs, Monument Valley Navajo Tribal Park

Overleaf: *Sandstone arch above West Canyon, west of Navajo Mountain*

"Near the summit I found an arrow sign . . . pointing off into the north toward those same old purple vistas, so grand, immense, and mysterious, of more canyons, more mesas and plateaus, more mountains, more cloud-dappled sun-spangled leagues of desert sand and desert rock, under the same old wide and aching sky." —Edward Abbey

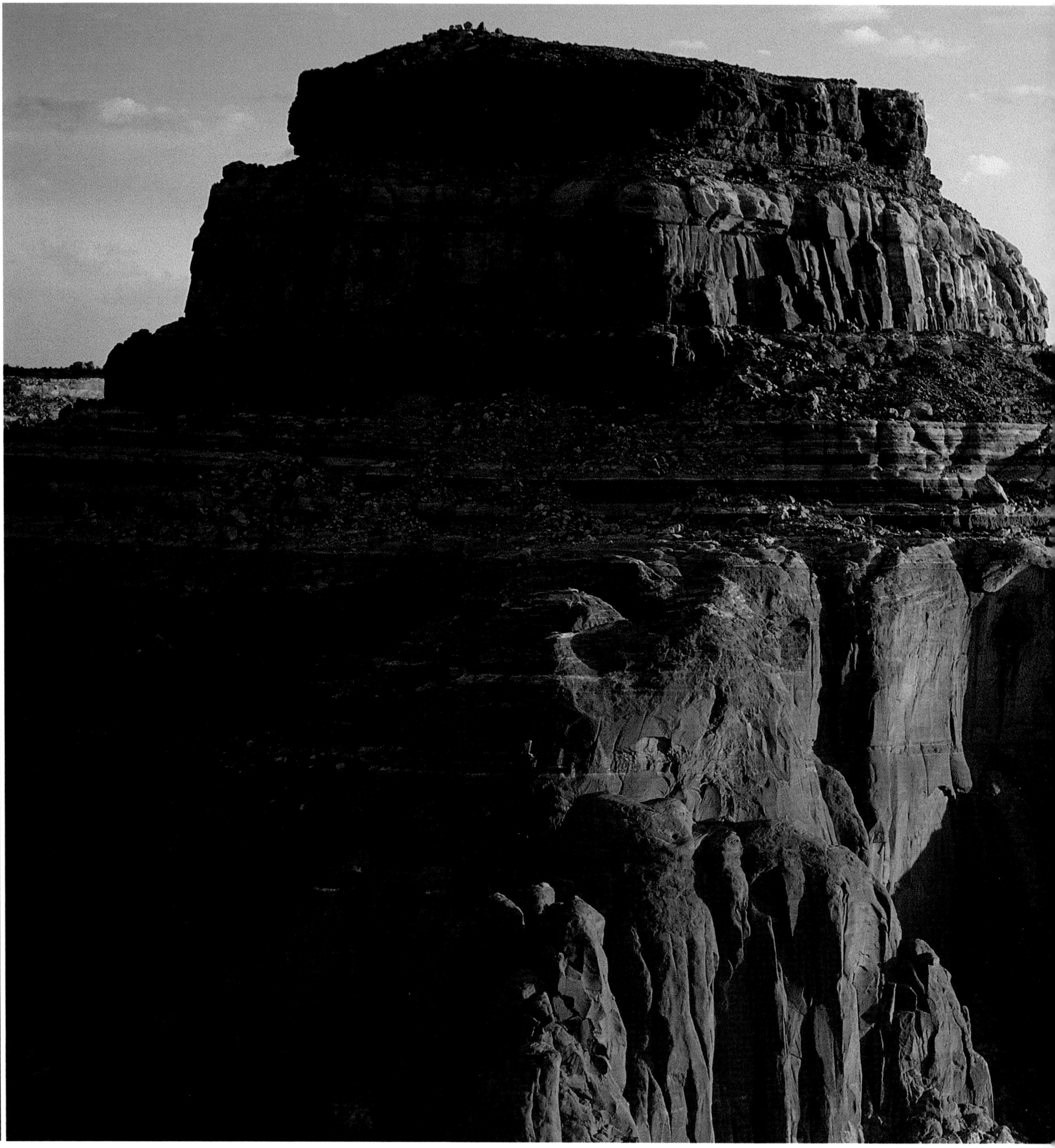

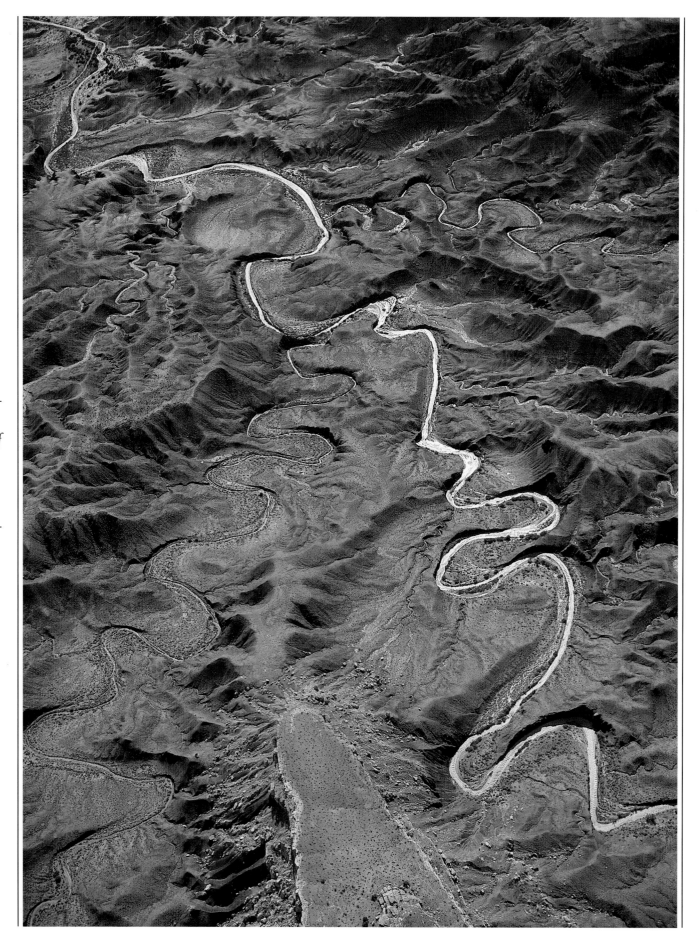

*D*rainage meanders of Moenkopi Wash, northeast of Tuba City

80

*G*rand Falls
on the Little
Colorado River,
southwestern   81
corner of the
Navajo Indian
Reservation

Early morning light on sheer cliffs, Monument Valley Navajo Tribal Park

Navajo Sandstone cliffs near Red Lake, north of Fort Defiance

"at dawn / Juniper takes another's sorrow in her hand
   a shard or splinter of red rock
     from arroyo bed or red dawn mountain
   to weigh against her own hard pain
     before the light is steady
   over calm mesas or abominations
     of far wars staining deserts
   similar to hers, staining
     other lives and agonies red-coral . . .

(continued on page 84)

Navajo Sandstone at the head of Buckskin Gulch, Paria Canyon Wilderness

*Chinle Formation along Newberry Mesa, north of
the Little Colorado River*

*. . . as the rock she flings up to
    today's uncaring peak runneled
by a fresh erosion of tears
    on cliff faces and faces accustomed
to tears; the suffering of others mighty,
    their sorrows weighty, outweighing her own
before the light is steady
    in Juniper's cupped hand humble and red
at dawn"* —Lucille Adler

*$\mathcal{P}$ainted Desert, south of Chinde Mesa, Petrified Forest
National Park*

"Night the mother, father fire
    Breed morning children in the dark.
Alone, she draws a cradle arc,
    Tucks in snow and braids a flame
To welcome their gold flickering,
    Then paints a sunrise on the floor . . .

S̶tormy sunrise, Little Colorado River Valley upriver
from Cameron

Overleaf: *Chinle Formation, north of Holbrook*

> *. . . With ochre, quartz and crimson ore,*
>   *Ground bone of owl and honeycomb—*
> *As conch and drumbeat tell the dawn*
>   *Why night and fire lie on stone,*
> *And she grows warm with child again."*
>   —*Lucille Adler*

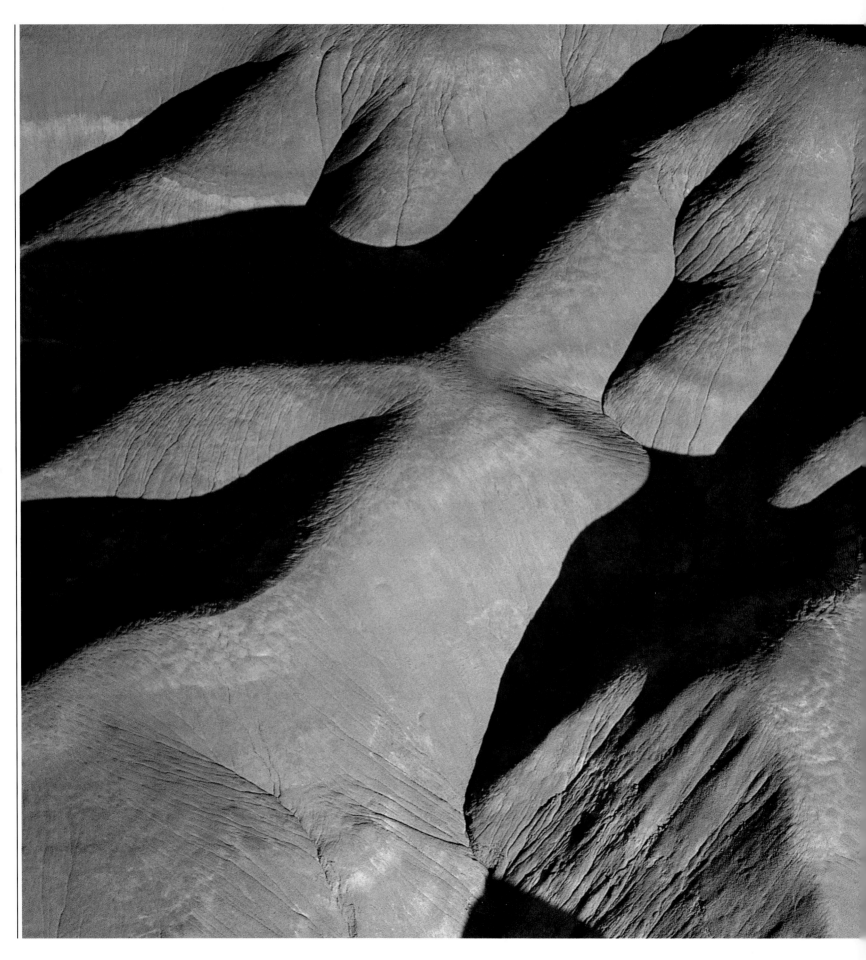

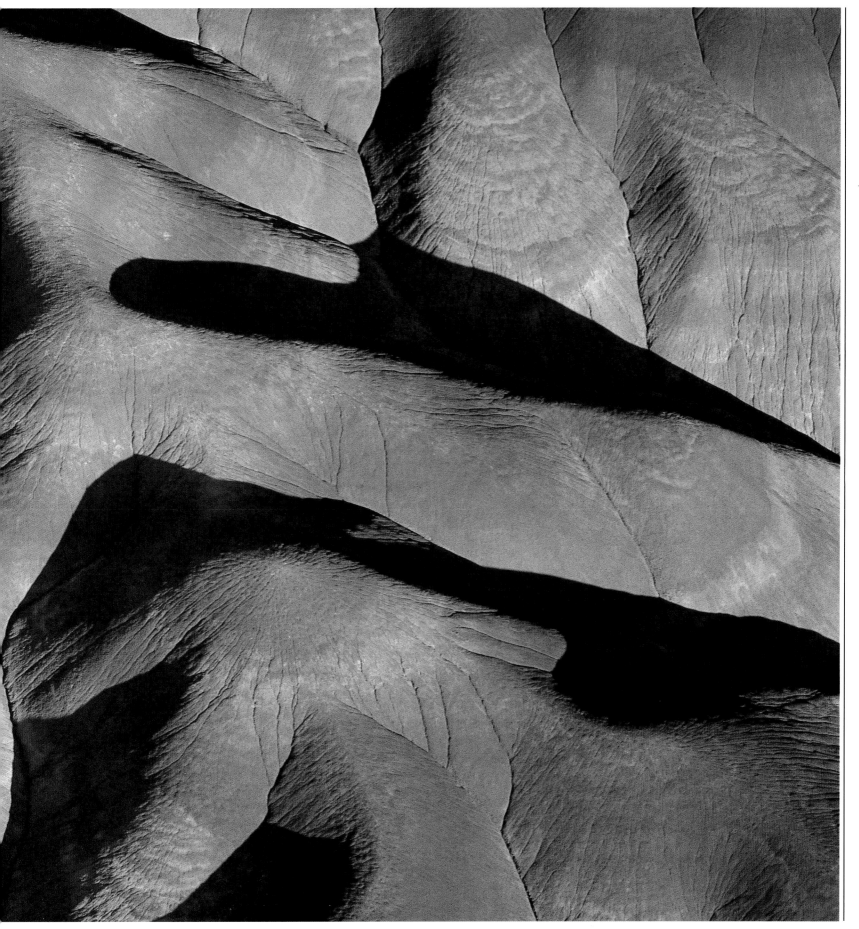

*S*and dunes along Hasbidito Creek, north of Lukachukai

Basalt cliff rises above forest, western Lukachukai Mountains

"When I say willows are dying
 by the dry stream beds
 and people are moving away
 I mean trees are dying
 everywhere and day by day
 water is sinking back
 to strata in the rock
 no one can reach . . .

(continued on page 92)

*C*inder cone amid the Hopi Buttes, near Dilkon

... and the people
   (they are what matters)
   the people like willow leaves
   coated with silver on one side
   lie too tarnished and dry
   for love, or to reach
   water drawing away
   out of reach everywhere ...

*Navajo Sandstone grids at the head of Buckskin Gulch,
Paria Canyon Wilderness*

*. . . what I mean falls
like a stone in the sand
where people and water
(they are what matters)
go on moving and drawing away
from each other farther
and deeper each day . . .*

(continued on page 94)

*S*and dunes at Comb Ridge, north of Kayenta

Painted Desert, south of Pilot Rock, Petrified Forest National Park

> . . . *and who will dive down*
>   *to find their sunken*
>   *silver ghosts together at last?*
>   *I mean who will be left*
>   *to drink a lonely toast*
>   *to all that mattered*
>   *around the glittering table in the dark?"*
>   —Lucille Adler, "The Level Eye"

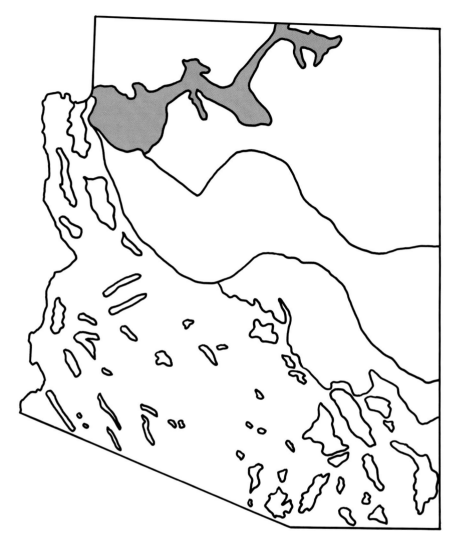

Canyon Country

Arizona has an elusive heart. For some, it lies within the Sonoran desert, panting beneath a palo verde. For others, it is found along the sycamore-lined creeks that tumble down from the state's oldest wilderness area in the Mazatzals. But for me, the heart of Arizona lies hidden somewhere in the canyon country, beneath the rims of the high deserts. After more than two years spent in the Grand Canyon, after trips into the sandstone cathedrals that once led to the inner sanctum of Glen Canyon, I am still searching. Perhaps someday, resting in the shade of a sandstone ledge deep within the Grand Canyon, I will stumble upon that heart.

The canyon country centers on the Colorado River in its headlong plunge off the Colorado Plateau. The river sculpted one canyon after another—Glen, Marble, Grand—in its search for sea level. The Little Colorado, cutting at a rate to keep pace with the main Colorado, carved a beautiful sheer canyon downstream from Cameron.

Canyons. The land can be flat for miles and suddenly, unannounced, be dissected into a maze with thousand-foot walls. As you walk down a creek bed, canyon walls rise up and drop away, rise up and drop away again. Is there rhyme or reason to this canyonscape? Yes, if you are willing to look deep enough. Underlying all of northern Arizona is the layer-cake geology of the Colorado Plateau. Sedimentary layers are stacked miles high above a basement of schist and granite. The layers have been bent and busted, folded and faulted. As water erodes into the surface, its behavior is always influenced by the preexisting layers and the folded, faulted forms that they have assumed. Creeks seek out the weakened zones of faulting, cut deeply into hard strata, broadly into soft strata. The end result is the infinitely varied topography and color of the canyon country.

Marble Canyon on the Colorado River, above 24-1/2-Mile Rapid, Grand Canyon National Park

*M*ain Street Valley, Shivwits Plateau

Sunlit ridge, eastern Grand Canyon National Park

"... I welcome the prospect of an army of lug-soled hiker's boots on the desert trails. To save what wilderness is left in the American Southwest—and in the American Southwest only the wilderness is worth saving—we are going to need all the recruits we can get. All the hands, heads, bodies, time, money, effort we can find." —Edward Abbey

*C̲ottonwoods along upper Navajo Canyon, west of Inscription
House Ruin, Navajo National Monument*

Trees changing to fall colors along Aztec Creek, southwest of Navajo Mountain

Overleaf: Dunes and cottonwoods along Aztec Creek, west of Navajo Mountain

*". . . those who learn to love what is spare, rough, wild,
undeveloped, and unbroken . . . will help resist the strip
miners, highway builders, land developers, weapons
testers, power producers, tree chainers, clear cutters, oil
drillers, dam beavers, subdividers . . . before that . . .
greedy crew succeeds in completely [destroying] . . . the
Great American Desert." —Edward Abbey*

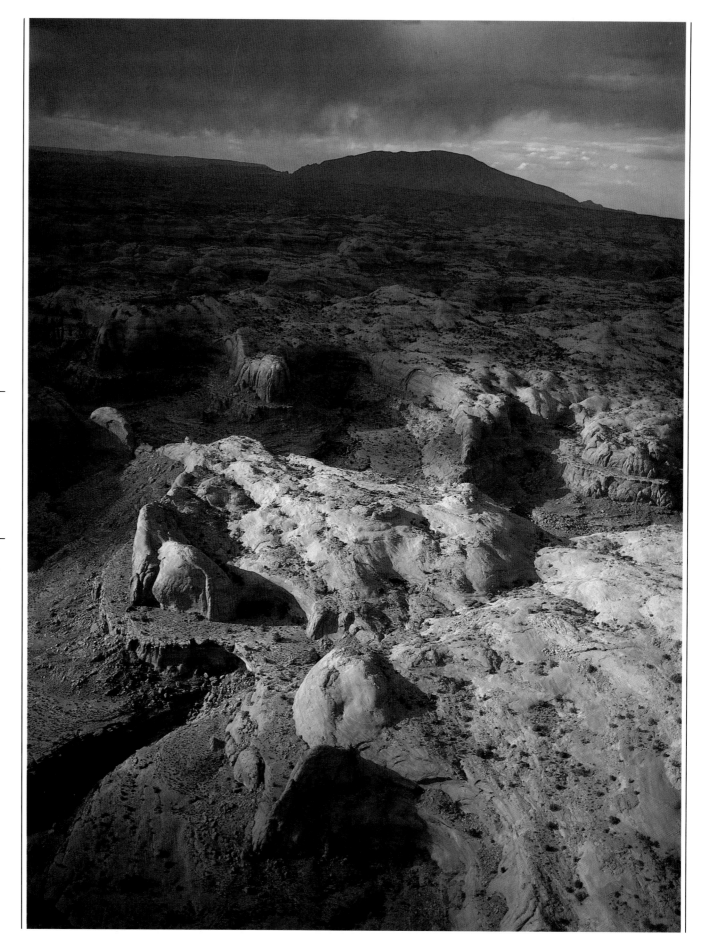

Rock formations in upper Navajo Canyon, south of Navajo Mountain

*C*liffs near
205-Mile
Canyon,   105
Grand Canyon
National Park

Whitmore Wash, Grand Canyon National Park

Cottonwoods along Navajo Creek, south of Navajo Mountain

"Each generation has its own rendezvous with the land, . . . we are all brief tenants on this planet. . . . We can misuse the land and diminish the usefulness of resources, or we can create a world in which physical affluence and affluence of the spirit go hand in hand."
—Stewart Udall

Marble Platform above North Canyon, Grand Canyon National Park

Joint patterns in the South Rim of the Grand Canyon, over National Canyon

109

*R*ainbow Bridge on the Arizona/Utah border, Glen Canyon
National Recreation Area

South Rim, western Grand Canyon National Park

"Here you may yet find the elemental freedom . . . to
experiment with solitude and stillness, to gaze through a
hundred miles of untrammeled atmosphere, across redrock
canyons, beyond blue mesas, toward the snow-covered
peaks of the most distant mountains—to make the
discovery of the self . . . which is not isolation but an
irreplaceable part of the mystery of the whole." —Edward Abbey

TECHNICAL INFORMATION

The photographs in this book were made with Pentax 645 cameras through 45mm, 75mm and 200mm Pentax lenses. A polarizing filter was used sparingly. Automatic metering was shutter-prioritized; exposures were made at 1/1,000 second whenever possible, but as slow as 1/125 second when necessary. Apertures were typically between f/2.8 and f/5.6. Fujichrome RDP 220 (ASA 100) color reversal film was used, with rare excursions back to Kodachrome PKR 120 (ASA 64). Imagecraft of Phoenix processed all of the film, frequently pushing the Fujichrome to an ASA of 200.

—M.C.

Cottonwoods and brush along Cienega Creek, southwest of Benson